DR JO LUKINS

Published by Turtle Publishing

©2022 Dr Jo Lukins

Dr Jo Lukins has asserted her right under the copyright, designs and patents act 1988 to be identified as the author of this work. The information in this book in based on the authors disclaims responsibility for any adverse consequences which may result from use of the information contained herein. Permission to use information has been sought by the author. Any breaches will be rectified in further editions of the book.

All rights reserved. No part of this publication may be reproduced, stored in or introduced into a retrieval system, or transmitted in any form, or by any means (electronic, mehcanical, photocopying, recording, or otherwise) without the prior written permission of the author.

The Game Plan is inspired by all those I know who have achieved greatness.

ON YOUR MARKS

The beginning is the *MOST IMPORTANT* part of the work

WELCOME TO YOUR GAME PLAN

Welcome and congratulations!

It's time. Time to elevate you from *good* to **great**. As success leaves clues, it is essential to use those clues on the pathway to excellence. With some consideration, planning and implementing the insights within this journal, you can think and achieve like a champion.

Making time and prioritising yourself to achieve excellence is your challenge. The temptation may be to move quickly through the information and the activities. However, I would encourage you to adopt patience. Good things take time, and whilst our world orients us towards quick results and life hacks, I promise you it will be worth it to take your time and make long-lasting results-focused changes.

This journal is your entry point into the Locker Room. A place where the wisdom of coaches and high performers have been tried and tested. Evidence-based strategies are detailed, and you are challenged to test what will work for you to move you closer to your goals. The strategies you need are here to accelerate your success. Once you know the key elements on how to formulate it, the game plan will be yours forever.

Let's get started.

GOAL COUNTDOWN

This is for your Big Hairy Audacious Goal (BHAG). If there is a key project you are working towards, write it in the middle of the countdown. Mark off it's due date, and then each day between now and then tick off a day and get a sense of progress as you move towards your goal.

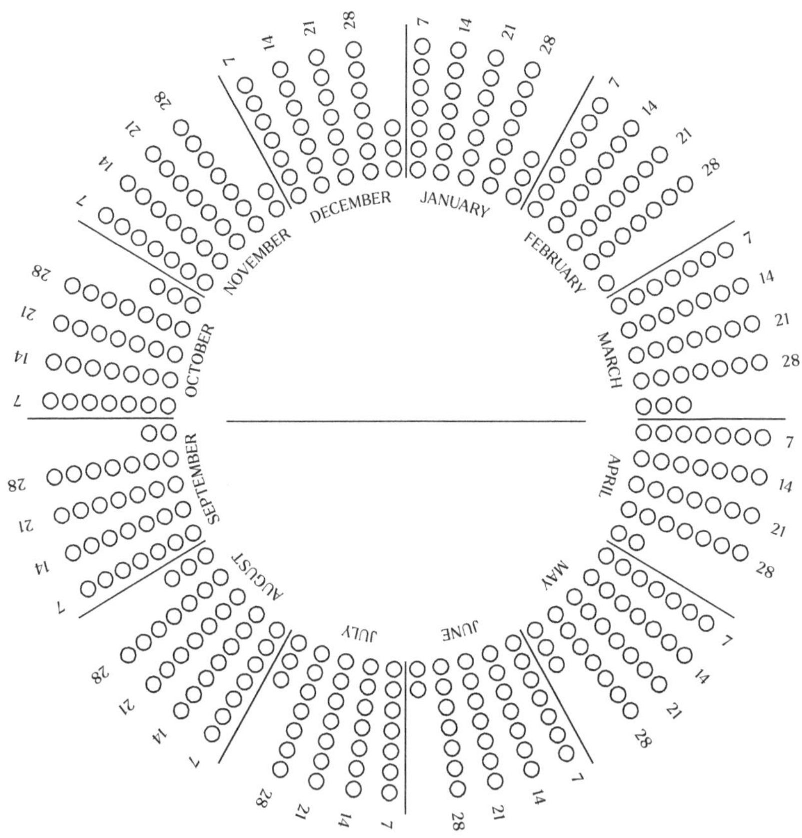

 For extra coaching on the countdown, scan here

THE PLAYBOOK

Long lasting success does not happen by accident.
Developing a Game Plan that will work requires 5 key steps:

>Reflection
>Education
>Practice
>Reflection
>Maintenance

You are a work in progress, building on your successes and the lessons you learn. The process is symbolised as a circle as we refine our expertise as we build wisdom.

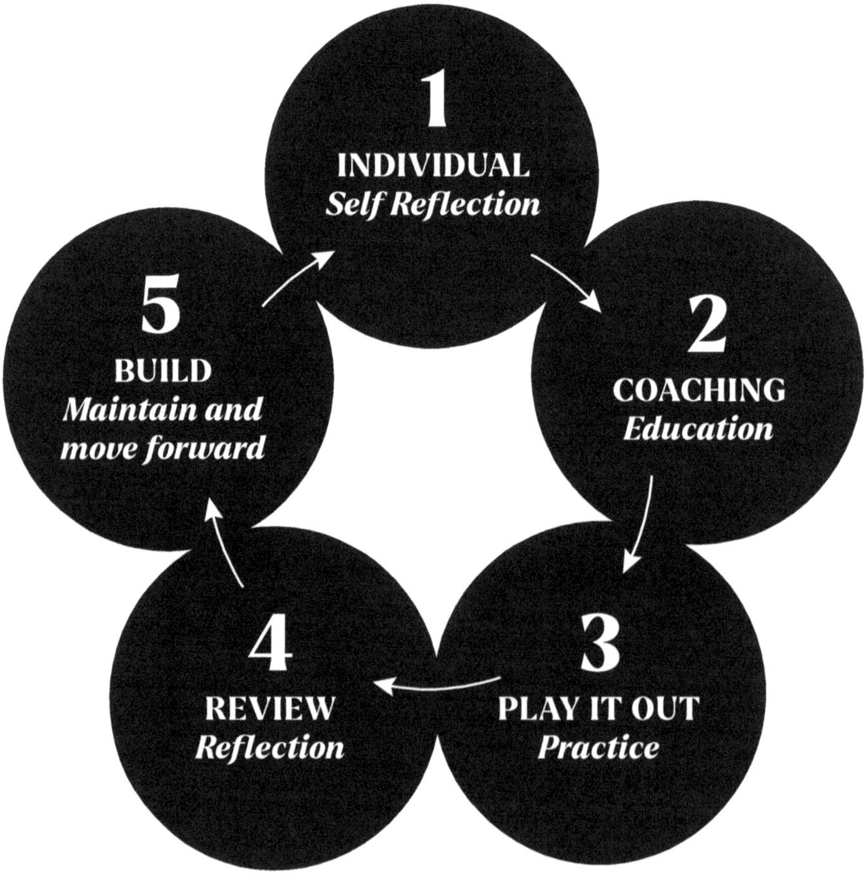

1 INDIVIDUAL *Self Reflection*
2 COACHING *Education*
3 PLAY IT OUT *Practice*
4 REVIEW *Reflection*
5 BUILD *Maintain and move forward*

YOUR TACTICS TO SUCCESS

"Strategy without tactics is the slowest route to victory. Tactics without strategy is the noise before defeat."

SUN TZU

Every game plan requires well considered strategy and tactics.
This is the outline of your journey.

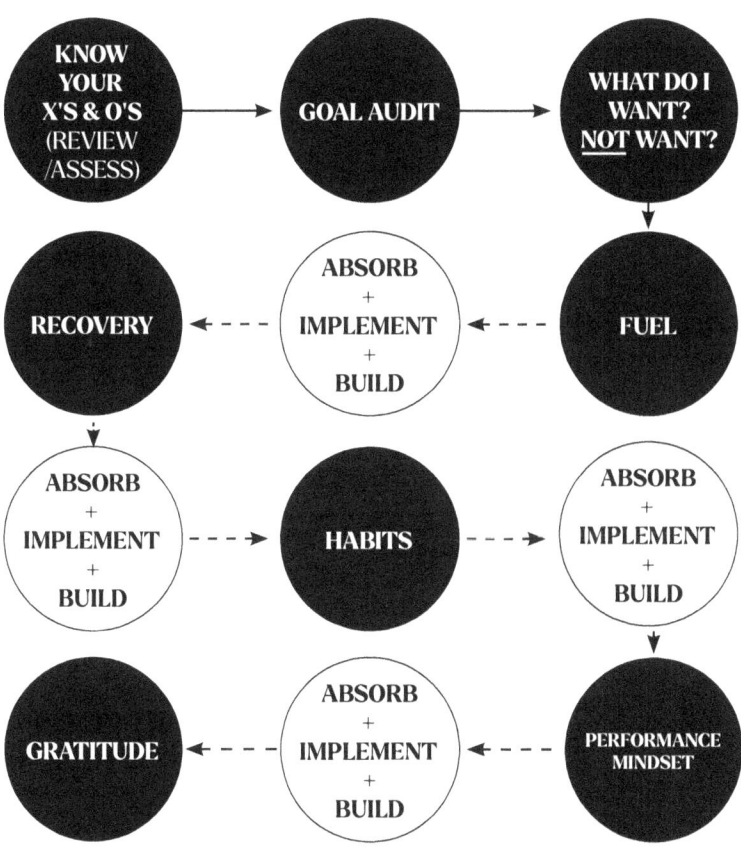

 Watch this video to discover more on your tactics for success.

NOTES

IN THE ZONE

"To know thyself is the beginning of wisdom"

SOCRATES

FULL STOP.

Let's draw a line in the sand. You CANNOT change anything until you acknowledge where you currently are. Only then can you move forward, but first you must understand where you have been.

"RIGHT HERE, RIGHT NOW"
FAT BOY SLIM

The questions on the following pages encourage you to circle the number that best captures how you rate that aspect of your life. Importantly, spend some time thinking why you have given it that number, and write down your reflections.

 To get you in the mood to write, you may want to scan this QR code to help you be present focused.

GOAL AUDIT

	Dissatisfied							Satisfied	

MY HEALTH 1 2 3 4 5 6 8 9 10
Why that rating?
_____
_____

MY FITNESS 1 2 3 4 5 6 8 9 10
Why that rating?
_____
_____

WORK (PAID/UNPAID) 1 2 3 4 5 6 8 9 10
Why that rating?
_____
_____

MONEY 1 2 3 4 5 6 8 9 10
Why that rating?
_____
_____

RELATIONSHIP 1 2 3 4 5 6 8 9 10
Why that rating?
_____
_____

CONFIDENCE 1 2 3 4 5 6 8 9 10
Why that rating?
_____
_____

MINDSET 1 2 3 4 5 6 8 9 10
Why that rating?
_____
_____

 To find out why we aren't including 7 within the rating scheme scan the QR code

 For extra coaching on this audit, scan here

Change happens best in increments. Wherever life is now, learn the clues of success and the lessons of disappointments. Whilst we can't always control our circumstances, we can control how we respond to it. Reflecting on the 5 questions below will increase your self-knowledge.

What are three highlights in your life that made you feel *grateful*, and why did they make you feel that way?

1. _____
2. _____
3. _____

What are three challenges or disappointments you have experienced, and what emotions did they create?

1. _____
2. _____
3. _____

What are three key lessons that life has taught you?

1. _____
2. _____
3. _____

What are three moments that make you feel proud, and why did they make you feel that way?

1. _____
2. _____
3. _____

Moving forward, what are three key goals or milestones you hope to achieve?

1. _____
2. _____
3. _____

NOTES

NOTES

ON THE PODIUM

"Success is nothing more than a few simple disciplines, practiced every day."

JIM ROHN

In each of the domains of your life, what is one thing you want to change or improve?

HEALTH_____

What excites you about making the change?

What concerns you about making the change?

FITNESS _____

What excites you about making the change?

What concerns you about making the change?

WORK (PAID/UNPAID) _____

What excites you about making the change?

What concerns you about making the change?

MONEY _____
What excites you about making the change?
_____
What concerns you about making the change?
_____

RELATIONSHIP _____
What excites you about making the change?
_____
What concerns you about making the change?
_____

CONFIDENCE _____
What excites you about making the change?
_____
What concerns you about making the change?
_____

MINDSET_____
What excites you about making the change?
_____
What concerns you about making the change?
_____

 For extra coaching on this exercise, scan here.

A year from now you will wish you had started today

KAREN LAMB

… FUEL

1 / MONTH ONE.

FUEL STOP

"Even the wisest people won't make good choices when they're not rested and their glucose is low."

ROY BAUMEISTER

 Set aside 30 minutes for this coaching session to kick off the month.

Would you like to take a challenge (and a memory test!)? Watch this video to find out how to take the Fuel Audit Challenge.

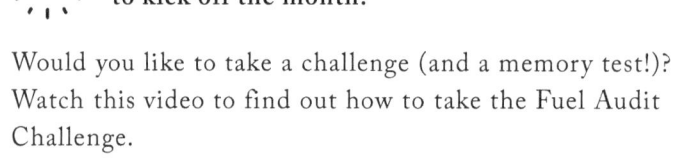

BREAKFAST		
MORNING TEA		
LUNCH		
AFTERNOON TEA		
DINNER		
AFTER DINNER		
CAFFINE DRINKS COFFEE/TEA/COKE		
WATER		

Remembering that success leaves clues, you've now considered the lessons from the last 24 hours. Let's not waste those valuable insights! Instead, list here your Golden Rules of Nutrition. These are the rules you have learnt about yourself, knowing what works for you, and want to follow moving forward. These will set the goalposts for you in making great choices in nutrition.

Now it's time to think about the changes you want to make. Consider your nutritional changes within this grid. List as many as you can, remembering we won't attempt to change too many at once!

 Watch this video to see how you can do this.

START	STOP
LESS	MORE

START	STOP
LESS	MORE

START	STOP
LESS	MORE

THIS MONTH

What will success look like for me this month, with my focus on fuel?

_____

_____

_____

_____

*"If you want to lift yourself up,
lift up someone else."*

BOOKER T. WASHINGTON

THIS WEEK

BIG 3

1. _____
2. _____
3. _____

FOUNDATIONS [fuel]

REVIEW + RESET

MY WINS

MY LEARNINGS

DATE   /   /

WHAT'S NEXT? [key target to conquer]

PERSONAL

PROFESSIONAL

WEEK 1

	KICK START	MAIN EVENT	EARLY EVENING	WIND DOWN
MON				
TUES				
WED				
THURS				
FRI				
SAT				
SUN				

NOTES

To find out how to use the weekly planners, scan here

WEEK 2

BIG 3 ———————————

1. _____
2. _____
3. _____

FOUNDATIONS [fuel]

_____
_____
_____
_____

REVIEW + RESET ———————

MY WINS

_____
_____
_____

MY LEARNINGS

_____
_____
_____

DATE   /   /

WHAT'S NEXT? [key target to conquer]

PERSONAL

PROFESSIONAL

WEEK 2

	KICK START	MAIN EVENT	EARLY EVENING	WIND DOWN
MON				
TUES				
WED				
THURS				
FRI				
SAT				
SUN				

NOTES

WEEK 3

BIG 3

1. _____
2. _____
3. _____

FOUNDATIONS [fuel]

_____
_____
_____
_____

REVIEW + RESET

MY WINS

_____
_____

MY LEARNINGS

_____
_____
_____

DATE   /   /

WHAT'S NEXT? [key target to conquer]

PERSONAL

PROFESSIONAL

WEEK 3

	KICK START	MAIN EVENT	EARLY EVENING	WIND DOWN
MON				
TUES				
WED				
THURS				
FRI				
SAT				
SUN				

NOTES

WEEK 4

BIG 3

1. _____
2. _____
3. _____

FOUNDATIONS [fuel]

_____
_____
_____
_____

REVIEW + RESET

MY WINS

_____
_____
_____

MY LEARNINGS

_____
_____
_____

DATE   /   /

WHAT'S NEXT? [key target to conquer]

PERSONAL

PROFESSIONAL

WEEK 4 / /

	KICK START	MAIN EVENT	EARLY EVENING	WIND DOWN
MON				
TUES				
WED				
THURS				
FRI				
SAT				
SUN				

NOTES

WEEK 5

BIG 3

1. _____
2. _____
3. _____

FOUNDATIONS [fuel]

_____
_____
_____
_____

REVIEW + RESET

MY WINS

_____
_____
_____

MY LEARNINGS

_____
_____
_____

DATE   /   /

WHAT'S NEXT? [key target to conquer]

PERSONAL

PROFESSIONAL

WEEK 5 /   /

	KICK START	MAIN EVENT	EARLY EVENING	WIND DOWN
MON				
TUES				
WED				
THURS				
FRI				
SAT				
SUN				

NOTES

"We are what we repeatedly do. Excellence, therefore, is not an act but a habit."

ARISTOTLE

2 / MONTH TWO.

REST

REST

"Remember that almost everything looks better after a good night's sleep"

H. JACKSON BROWN JR.

Sleep can be our best friend or our worst enemy. When it comes to performance, we can utilise sleep as one of our most significant training partners. Vital for attention, concentration, memory and recovery, a performance plan for sleep is essential.

There is no golden number for how many hours of sleep you need. However for most, the Goldilocks 'sweet spot' is between 7-9 hours. There is nothing heroic in living in constant sleep deprivation. Far better that you thrive with sufficient rest.

Despite the need for longer, most adults get about 6.5 hours of sleep per night. Sleep loss accumulates into sleep debt. Over a 5-day workweek, a nightly sleep loss of 90 minutes builds into a 7.5-hour sleep debt by the weekend. Losing 2 hours of sleep a night (sleeping 6 hours instead of 8) significantly impairs performance, attention, working memory, long-term memory and decision making.

Research has shown that having 6 hours of sleep when you normally average 8 hours, impacts your performance in the same way it would if you had drunk two or three beers – while losing 4 hours of sleep equated to effects comparable to those with a 0.1% breath alcohol measurement.

It will be challenging to improve any functioning when the symptoms of poor sleep are present.

Give the effects of quality sleep, *imagine how getting 60-120 minutes more could improve performance?*

Let's get a gauge on your current sleeping behaviours to identify areas that can be improved. If you understand where your sleep is most often impacted, it can guide you towards the strategies that will help you improve your sleep and your performance.

1. How long does it typically take you to fall asleep?

0-15 min	16-30 min	31-45 min	46-60 min	>60min
4 points	3 points	2 points	1 point	0 points

2. If you wake up during the night, approximately how long are you awake in total?

0-15 min	16-30 min	31-45 min	46-60 min	>60min
4 points	3 points	2 points	1 point	0 points

3. If you wake-up before you intend to wake up, how much earlier is this?

I don't wake up too early (Up to 15min early)	4 points
16-30 min early	3 points
31-45 min early	2 points
46-60 min early	1 point
>60 min early	0 points

4. How many nights a week do you have a problem with your sleep?

0-1	2	3	4	5-7
4 points	3 points	2 points	1 point	0 points

5. How would you rate your overall sleep quality?

Very good	Good	Average	Poor	Very poor
4 points	3 points	2 points	1 point	0 points

Thinking about the past month, to what extent has poor sleep...

6. affected your mood, energy, or relationships?

Not at all	A little	Somewhat	Much	Very much
4 points	3 points	2 points	1 point	0 points

7. affected your concentration, productivity, or ability to stay awake?

Not at all	A little	Somewhat	Much	Very much
4 points	3 points	2 points	1 point	0 points

8. troubled you in general?

Not at all	A little	Somewhat	Much	Very much
4 points	3 points	2 points	1 point	0 points

9. how long have you had a problem with your sleep?

Not at all	1-2 months	3-6 months	7-12 months	More than a year
4 points	3 points	2 points	1 point	0 points

Add up your score _____

 The next step is to read this guide to get the steps you can take towards improving your sleep

My top sleep tips:

1_____
2_____
3_____
4_____
5_____

NOTES

THIS MONTH

What will success look like for me this month, with my focus on sleep recovery?

_____

_____

_____

_____

_____

"Challenges are what make life interesting and overcoming them is what makes life meaningful."

JOSHUA J. MARINE

RECOVERY RECORD

Quality score ☹ 1 2 3 4 5 ☺

To find out how to best use this record, watch here.

Quality																																			
6pm																																			
7pm																																			
8pm																																			
9pm																																			
10pm																																			
11pm																																			
12pm																																			
1am																																			
2am																																			
3am																																			
4am																																			
5am																																			
6am																																			
7am																																			
8am																																			
9am																																			
	S	M	T	W	T	F	S	S	M	T	W	T	F	S	S	M	T	W	T	F	S	S	M	T	W	T	F	S	S	M	T	W	T	F	S

WEEK 1

BIG 3

1. _____
2. _____
3. _____

FOUNDATIONS [fuel, rest]

_____
_____
_____
_____

REVIEW + RESET

MY WINS

_____
_____
_____

MY LEARNINGS

_____
_____
_____

DATE / /

WHAT'S NEXT? [key target to conquer]

PERSONAL

PROFESSIONAL

WEEK 1

	KICK START	MAIN EVENT	EARLY EVENING	WIND DOWN
MON				
TUES				
WED				
THURS				
FRI				
SAT				
SUN				

NOTES

WEEK 2

BIG 3 ───────────

1. _____
2. _____
3. _____

FOUNDATIONS [fuel, rest]

_____
_____
_____
_____

REVIEW + RESET ───────────

MY WINS

_____
_____
_____

MY LEARNINGS

_____
_____
_____

DATE ___ / ___ / _____

WHAT'S NEXT? [key target to conquer]

_____
_____
_____
_____
_____
_____
_____

PERSONAL

_____
_____
_____

PROFESSIONAL

_____
_____
_____

WEEK 2

	KICK START	MAIN EVENT	EARLY EVENING	WIND DOWN
MON				
TUES				
WED				
THURS				
FRI				
SAT				
SUN				

WEEK 3

BIG 3

1. _____
2. _____
3. _____

FOUNDATIONS [fuel, rest]

_____

_____

_____

_____

REVIEW + RESET

MY WINS

_____

_____

MY LEARNINGS

_____

_____

DATE   /   /

WHAT'S NEXT? [key target to conquer]

PERSONAL

PROFESSIONAL

WEEK 3

	KICK START	MAIN EVENT	EARLY EVENING	WIND DOWN
MON				
TUES				
WED				
THURS				
FRI				
SAT				
SUN				

NOTES

WEEK 4

BIG 3

1. _____
2. _____
3. _____

FOUNDATIONS [fuel, rest]

_____
_____
_____
_____

REVIEW + RESET

MY WINS

_____
_____
_____

MY LEARNINGS

_____
_____
_____

DATE   /   /

WHAT'S NEXT? [key target to conquer]

PERSONAL

PROFESSIONAL

WEEK 4

	KICK START	MAIN EVENT	EARLY EVENING	WIND DOWN
MON				
TUES				
WED				
THURS				
FRI				
SAT				
SUN				

NOTES

WEEK 5

BIG 3 ──────────────

1. ─────────────────────────────
2. ─────────────────────────────
3. ─────────────────────────────

FOUNDATIONS [fuel, rest]

─────────────────────────────────
─────────────────────────────────
─────────────────────────────────
─────────────────────────────────

REVIEW + RESET ──────────

MY WINS

─────────────────────────────────
─────────────────────────────────
─────────────────────────────────

MY LEARNINGS

─────────────────────────────────
─────────────────────────────────
─────────────────────────────────

DATE   /   /

WHAT'S NEXT? [key target to conquer]

_____
_____
_____
_____
_____
_____
_____
_____

PERSONAL

_____
_____
_____

PROFESSIONAL

_____
_____
_____

WEEK 5

	KICK START	MAIN EVENT	EARLY EVENING	WIND DOWN
MON				
TUES				
WED				
THURS				
FRI				
SAT				
SUN				

NOTES

"The most difficult thing is
the decision to act,
the rest is merely tenacity."

AMELIA EARHART

3 / MONTH THREE.

HABITS

HABITS

"Quality is not an act; it is a habit."

ARISTOTLE

 Set aside 30 minutes for this coaching session to kick off the month.

By the time you sip on your first morning coffee, you are likely to have already made more than 1,000 decisions. In fact, by the end of the day, it is estimated that most adults have made around 35,000 conscious decisions. Whilst that reads a large number, research from Cornell University determine people average 226.7 decisions per day on food alone!

The truth about habits – they are great, because they save us from having to think. They are also terrible, because they save us from having to think! You create your habits, and then your habits will control your life.

Remember:
You are not always motivated... so you need to learn discipline.
You will not always be disciplined... so you need to develop habits.

 Are you ready to begin? Let's automate some of those good intentions for you. First, watch this video for the 'how to' of habit success.

How can you create helpful habits in your life?

1. Identify a target behaviour and pick a small habit to change
   (e.g. taking your multivitamin regularly; making more eye contact in conversations, flossing, or tidying your desk at the end of the day).
2. Consider why you haven't already been doing this behaviour.
3. Ask yourself why you are now ready to change.?
4. Articulate the when/then.
5. Write down your when/then behaviour.
6. Monitor your progress.

FORMING NEW HABITS ACTIVITY

WHAT WILL I STOP OR CHANGE	THESE HABITS OCCUR BECAUSE...

WHAT I WILL DO NOW MOVING FORWARD...	THE POSITIVE IMPACT FOR ME WILL BE...

Notes:
_____
_____
_____
_____
_____
_____
_____
_____
_____

HOW CAN YOU CREATE HELPFUL HABITS IN YOUR LIFE?

1. Identify a target behaviour and pick a small habit change (e.g. lowering the toilet seat, pausing before responding, making eye contact, listening well or tracking cash flow).

   _____
   _____
   _____

2. Consider why you haven't already been doing this behaviour.

   _____
   _____
   _____

3. Ask yourself why you are now ready to change.

   _____
   _____
   _____

4. Articulate the when/then.

   _____
   _____
   _____

5. Write down your when/then behaviour.

   _____
   _____
   _____

6. Monitor your progress.

   _____
   _____
   _____

HOW CAN YOU CREATE HELPFUL HABITS IN YOUR LIFE?

1. Identify a target behaviour and pick a small habit change (e.g. lowering the toilet seat, pausing before responding, making eye contact, listening well or tracking cash flow).

2. Consider why you haven't already been doing this behaviour.

3. Ask yourself why you are now ready to change.

4. Articulate the when/then.

5. Write down your when/then behaviour.

6. Monitor your progress.

THIS MONTH

What will success look like for me this month, with my focus on habits?

_____

_____

_____

_____

_____

The person who says it cannot be done should not interrupt the person who is doing it.

CHINESE PROVERB

RECOVERY RECORD

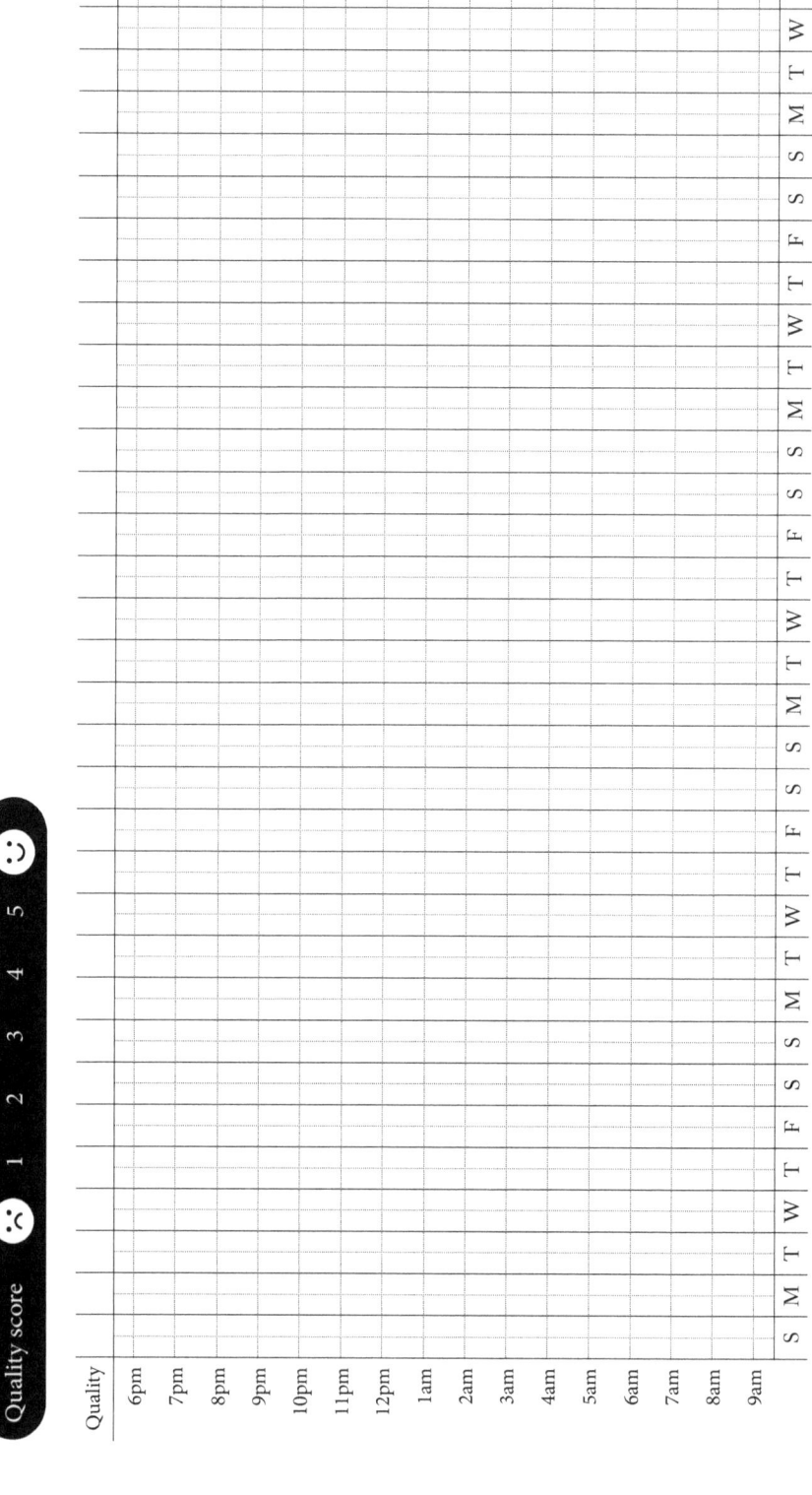

30 DAY HABIT STREAK

To find out how to best record your 30 day habit streak, watch here.

				M
				T
				W
				T
				F
				S
				S
				M
				T
				W
				T
				F
				S
				S
				M
				T
				W
				T
				F
				S
				S
				M
				T
				W
				T
				F
				S
				S
				M
				T
				W

WEEK 1

BIG 3

1. _____
2. _____
3. _____

FOUNDATIONS [fuel, rest, habits]

_____
_____
_____
_____

REVIEW + RESET

MY WINS

_____
_____

MY LEARNINGS

_____
_____

DATE / /

WHAT'S NEXT? [key target to conquer]

_____
_____
_____
_____
_____
_____
_____

PERSONAL

_____
_____
_____

PROFESSIONAL

_____
_____
_____

WEEK 1

	KICK START	MAIN EVENT	EARLY EVENING	WIND DOWN
MON				
TUES				
WED				
THURS				
FRI				
SAT				
SUN				

NOTES

WEEK 2

BIG 3

1. _____
2. _____
3. _____

FOUNDATIONS [fuel, rest, habits]

_____
_____
_____
_____

REVIEW + RESET

MY WINS

_____
_____
_____

MY LEARNINGS

_____
_____
_____

DATE   /   /

WHAT'S NEXT? [key target to conquer]

PERSONAL

PROFESSIONAL

WEEK 2

	KICK START	MAIN EVENT	EARLY EVENING	WIND DOWN
MON				
TUES				
WED				
THURS				
FRI				
SAT				
SUN				

NOTES

/
WEEK 3
/

BIG 3 ───────────────

1. _____

2. _____

3. _____

FOUNDATIONS [fuel, rest, habits]

_____

_____

_____

_____

REVIEW + RESET ───────────

MY WINS

_____

_____

_____

MY LEARNINGS

_____

_____

_____

DATE   /   /
___

WHAT'S NEXT? [key target to conquer]

PERSONAL

PROFESSIONAL

WEEK 3   /   /

	KICK START	MAIN EVENT	EARLY EVENING	WIND DOWN
MON				
TUES				
WED				
THURS				
FRI				
SAT				
SUN				

WEEK 4

BIG 3

1. _____
2. _____
3. _____

FOUNDATIONS [fuel, rest, habits]

_____
_____
_____
_____

REVIEW + RESET

MY WINS

_____
_____
_____

MY LEARNINGS

_____
_____
_____

DATE   /   /

WHAT'S NEXT? [key target to conquer]

PERSONAL

PROFESSIONAL

WEEK 4

	KICK START	MAIN EVENT	EARLY EVENING	WIND DOWN
MON				
TUES				
WED				
THURS				
FRI				
SAT				
SUN				

NOTES

/ WEEK 5 /

BIG 3 ———————————————

1. _____
2. _____
3. _____

FOUNDATIONS [fuel, rest, habits]

_____
_____
_____
_____

REVIEW + RESET ———————————

MY WINS

_____
_____
_____

MY LEARNINGS

_____
_____
_____

DATE   /   /

WHAT'S NEXT? [key target to conquer]

PERSONAL

PROFESSIONAL

WEEK 5   /   /

	KICK START	MAIN EVENT	EARLY EVENING	WIND DOWN
MON				
TUES				
WED				
THURS				
FRI				
SAT				
SUN				

NOTES

> *"Every strike brings me closer to the next home run."*
>
> — BABE RUTH

4 / MONTH FOUR.

MINDSET

PERFORMANCE MINDSET

"If my mind can conceive it, and my heart can believe it – then I can achieve it."

MUHAMMAD ALI

A performance mindset is the foundation to believing you can improve at anything if you try and are mentally prepared for success. When you choose to view the world through a performance mindset, you are more likely to consider your potential rather than be limited by your current ability.

When you can see the opportunity to improve, grow and learn, you are more likely to achieve with engagement. In addition, when you view the world through the perspective of growth, you handle disappointment and failure better. A performance mindset will help you in many ways – in study, work, sport, health and in your relationships

 Is your thinking based on a fixed or performance mindset?
What is your mindset? Take this quick quiz to find out.

1. I believe that talent is something you are born with and you either have it or you don't.	TRUE	FALSE	
2. The chance to show others your ability is a key source of your motivation.	TRUE	FALSE	
3. When you are talented, things will come more easily to you.	TRUE	FALSE	
4. It is better to do the things you are successful at than to appear less talented.	TRUE	FALSE	
5. When you don't achieve in something, it is confirmation there are some things that you just simply won't be good at.	TRUE	FALSE	
6. I give my attention to the things I am good at and don't want to focus on negative feedback.	TRUE	FALSE	
7. Sometimes things just don't work out and that is not your fault.	TRUE	FALSE	
SCORING: TRUE = 0 points, FALSE = 1 point	TOTAL		

Your score will rate between 0 and 7. The higher you score the more you think with a performance mindset, which will maximise your potential. The lower your score, the greater the likelihood that you will plateau early and under achieve.

There's a good chance that if you've scored lower, you will react with a fixed mindset and be concerned you have 'failed' this test. No! This isn't a test to pass or fail, but rather an indicator of where your thinking is at now. Just by knowing there are alternative ways of thinking, you open up the possibility for change, which can then help you to achieve things you previously didn't think possible.

The key understanding of a performance mindset is that every training session, work meeting, parenting moment, or time spent on a project, is an opportunity to learn, execute strategy and evaluate your performance.

 For this month's challenge, watch this video to learn how to undertake a post-performance review.

> *"If you put forth the effort, good things will be bestowed upon you."*
>
> MICHAEL JORDAN

THIS MONTH

What will success look like for me this month, with my focus on mindset?

_____

_____

_____

_____

_____

"There are no traffic jams along the extra mile."

ROGER STAUBACH

RECOVERY RECORD

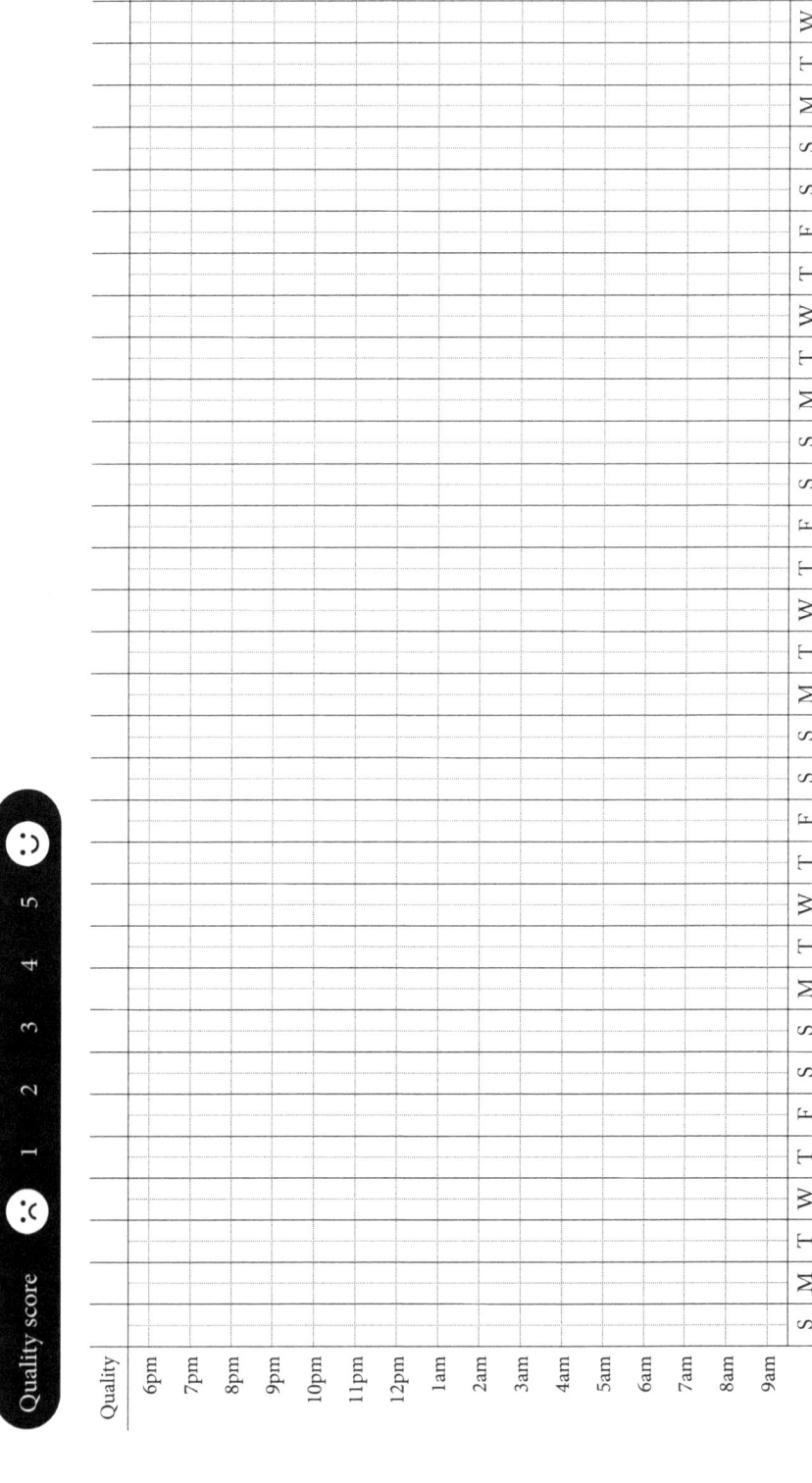

30 DAY HABIT STREAK

	1	2	3	4
M				
T				
W				
T				
F				
S				
S				
M				
T				
W				
T				
F				
S				
S				
M				
T				
W				
T				
F				
S				
S				
M				
T				
W				
T				
F				
S				
S				
M				
T				
W				
T				
F				
S				

WEEK 1

BIG 3 ———————————————

1. _____
2. _____
3. _____

FOUNDATIONS [fuel, rest, habits, mindset]

_____
_____
_____
_____

REVIEW + RESET ———————————

MY WINS

_____
_____
_____

MY LEARNINGS

_____
_____
_____

DATE   /   /

WHAT'S NEXT? [key target to conquer]

PERSONAL

PROFESSIONAL

WEEK 1

	KICK START	MAIN EVENT	EARLY EVENING	WIND DOWN
MON				
TUES				
WED				
THURS				
FRI				
SAT				
SUN				

NOTES

/
WEEK 2
/

BIG 3 ———————————————

1. _____
2. _____
3. _____

FOUNDATIONS [fuel, rest, habits]

_____
_____
_____
_____

REVIEW + RESET ———————————

MY WINS

_____
_____
_____

MY LEARNINGS

_____
_____
_____

DATE / /

WHAT'S NEXT? [key target to conquer]

PERSONAL

PROFESSIONAL

WEEK 2 /   /

	KICK START	MAIN EVENT	EARLY EVENING	WIND DOWN
MON				
TUES				
WED				
THURS				
FRI				
SAT				
SUN				

WEEK 3

BIG 3

1. _____
2. _____
3. _____

FOUNDATIONS [fuel, rest, habits]

_____
_____
_____
_____

REVIEW + RESET

MY WINS

_____
_____
_____

MY LEARNINGS

_____
_____
_____

DATE   /   /

WHAT'S NEXT? [key target to conquer]

PERSONAL

PROFESSIONAL

WEEK 3

	KICK START	MAIN EVENT	EARLY EVENING	WIND DOWN
MON				
TUES				
WED				
THURS				
FRI				
SAT				
SUN				

NOTES

WEEK 4

BIG 3 ——————————————

1. _____

2. _____

3. _____

FOUNDATIONS [fuel, rest, habits]

_____

_____

_____

_____

REVIEW + RESET ——————————

MY WINS

_____

_____

_____

MY LEARNINGS

_____

_____

_____

DATE   /   /

WHAT'S NEXT? [key target to conquer]

PERSONAL

PROFESSIONAL

WEEK 4

	KICK START	MAIN EVENT	EARLY EVENING	WIND DOWN
MON				
TUES				
WED				
THURS				
FRI				
SAT				
SUN				

WEEK 5

BIG 3 ———————————————

1. _____
2. _____
3. _____

FOUNDATIONS [fuel, rest, habits]

_____
_____
_____
_____

REVIEW + RESET ———————————

MY WINS

_____
_____

MY LEARNINGS

_____
_____

DATE _____ / ____ / _____

WHAT'S NEXT? [key target to conquer]

_____
_____
_____
_____
_____
_____
_____
_____

PERSONAL

_____
_____
_____

PROFESSIONAL

_____
_____
_____

WEEK 5

	KICK START	MAIN EVENT	EARLY EVENING	WIND DOWN
MON				
TUES				
WED				
THURS				
FRI				
SAT				
SUN				

*The best time to plant a tree was 20 years ago.
The second-best time is now.*

CHINESE PROVERB

5 / MONTH FIVE.

GRATITUDE

GRATITUDE

*"Gratitude can transform common days into thanksgivings,
turn routine jobs into joy,
and change ordinary opportunities into blessings."*

WILLIAM ARTHUR WARD

 Set aside 30 minutes for this coaching session to kick off the month.

A body of evidence is growing to show that gratitude can contribute to improving athletic performance. It works on performance by facilitating sleep, reducing stress, boosting self-esteem and increasing life satisfaction. The bottom line is, when you include more gratitude in your life the benefits will flow out like ripples on a pond.

Gratitude is a moment of reflection which gives you greater clarity. It also helps you redefine failure and disappointment and is beneficial in cultivating a growth mindset. Did you know that telling someone you appreciate them can increase your own happiness by about 15%? In contrast if you lack gratitude, you'll often be less productive and effective in the things that you do. A lack of gratitude has a fatiguing effect (on you and those around you).

Did you know?!

A fascinating study conducted in the United States had healthy participants come into the laboratory and complete a happiness questionnaire. They were then administered a rhinovirus (the most common form of the cold) via nasal drops. Placed into quarantine for five days in a hotel, the volunteers were subsequently followed for a further four weeks. The research demonstrated that happier participants were less likely to develop a cold, and if they did, it didn't last as long as their less happy counterparts!

Feeling brave? Try this exercise!

Pick an aspect of your life (work, personal, relationships, sport) and list 7 things you have to do in relation to that area.

I have to_____

I have to_____

I have to_____

I have to_____

I have to_____

I have to_____

I have to_____

 To complete part b of this exercise, you need to watch this short video.

NOTES

THIS MONTH

What will success look like for me this month, with my focus on gratitude?

_____

_____

_____

_____

_____

"Remember that not getting what you want is sometimes a wonderful stroke of luck."

DALAI LAMA

RECOVERY RECORD

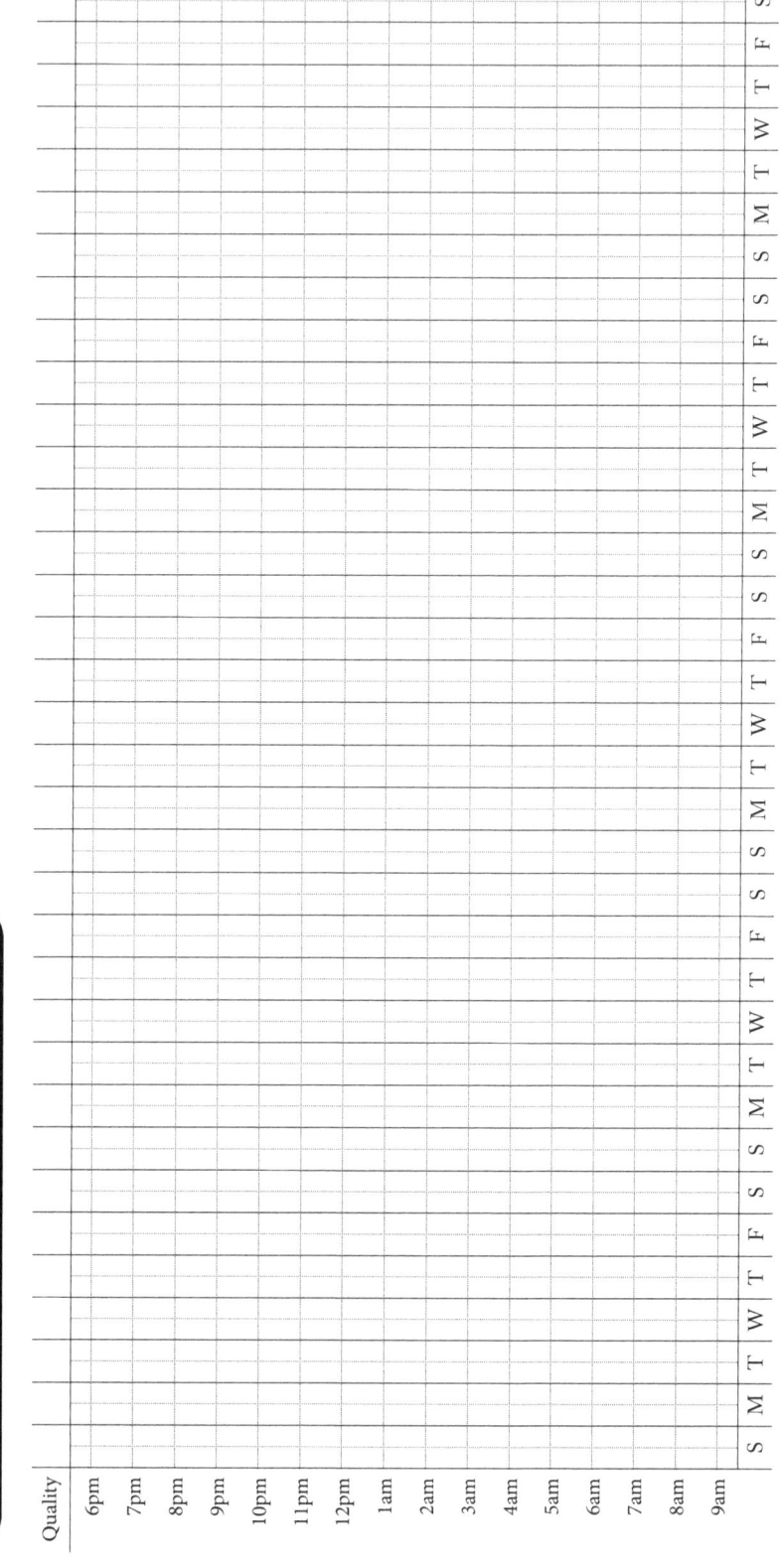

30 DAY HABIT STREAK

	M	T	W	T	F	S	S	M	T	W	T	F	S	S	M	T	W	T	F	S	S	M	T	W	T	F	S	S	M	T
1																														
2																														
3																														
4																														

30 DAYS OF GRATITUDE

To find out how to best utilise your 30 days of gratitude, watch here.

1.	16.
2.	17.
3.	18.
4.	19.
5.	20.
6.	21.
7.	22.
8.	23.
9.	24.
10.	25.
11.	26.
12.	27.
13.	28.
14.	29.
15.	30.

A 30-day journal of gratitude has been shown to increase happiness, reduce symptoms of mild depression, and place people closer to their performance goals. The back of this journal includes a bonus 6 months of gratitude recording (you're welcome!).

WEEK 1

BIG 3 ———————————————

1. _____
2. _____
3. _____

FOUNDATIONS [fuel, rest, habits, mindset, gratitude]

_____
_____
_____
_____

REVIEW + RESET ————————————

MY WINS

_____
_____
_____

MY LEARNINGS

_____
_____
_____

DATE   /   /

WHAT'S NEXT? [key target to conquer]

_____
_____
_____
_____
_____
_____
_____
_____

PERSONAL

_____
_____
_____

PROFESSIONAL

_____
_____
_____

WEEK 1   / /

	KICK START	MAIN EVENT	EARLY EVENING	WIND DOWN
MON				
TUES				
WED				
THURS				
FRI				
SAT				
SUN				

NOTES

WEEK 2

BIG 3 ———————————————

1. _____
2. _____
3. _____

FOUNDATIONS [fuel, rest, habits, mindset, gratitude]

_____
_____
_____
_____

REVIEW + RESET ———————————

MY WINS

_____
_____
_____

MY LEARNINGS

_____
_____
_____

DATE   /   /

WHAT'S NEXT? [key target to conquer]

_____
_____
_____
_____
_____
_____
_____

PERSONAL

_____
_____
_____

PROFESSIONAL

_____
_____
_____

WEEK 2   /   /

	KICK START	MAIN EVENT	EARLY EVENING	WIND DOWN
MON				
TUES				
WED				
THURS				
FRI				
SAT				
SUN				

NOTES

WEEK 3

BIG 3 ———————————————

1. _____
2. _____
3. _____

FOUNDATIONS [fuel, rest, habits, mindset, gratitude]

_____
_____
_____
_____

REVIEW + RESET ———————————

MY WINS

_____
_____
_____

MY LEARNINGS

_____
_____
_____

DATE   /   /

WHAT'S NEXT? [key target to conquer]

PERSONAL

PROFESSIONAL

WEEK 3

	KICK START	MAIN EVENT	EARLY EVENING	WIND DOWN
MON				
TUES				
WED				
THURS				
FRI				
SAT				
SUN				

NOTES

WEEK 4

BIG 3

1. _____
2. _____
3. _____

FOUNDATIONS [fuel, rest, habits, mindset, gratitude]

_____
_____
_____
_____

REVIEW + RESET

MY WINS

_____
_____

MY LEARNINGS

_____
_____

DATE   /   /

WHAT'S NEXT? [key target to conquer]

_____
_____
_____
_____
_____
_____
_____

PERSONAL

_____
_____

PROFESSIONAL

_____
_____

WEEK 4

	KICK START	MAIN EVENT	EARLY EVENING	WIND DOWN
MON				
TUES				
WED				
THURS				
FRI				
SAT				
SUN				

NOTES

/ WEEK 5 /

BIG 3

1. _____
2. _____
3. _____

FOUNDATIONS [fuel, rest, habits, mindset, gratitude]

_____
_____
_____
_____

REVIEW + RESET

MY WINS

_____
_____
_____

MY LEARNINGS

_____
_____
_____

DATE   /   /

WHAT'S NEXT? [key target to conquer]

___

PERSONAL

___

PROFESSIONAL

WEEK 5   / /

	KICK START	MAIN EVENT	EARLY EVENING	WIND DOWN
MON				
TUES				
WED				
THURS				
FRI				
SAT				
SUN				

NOTES

Congratulations!

5 MONTHS OF FOCUS ON
YOUR GAME PLAN.

TO FIND OUT YOUR NEXT MOVE.
SCAN HERE

WWW.DRJOLUKINS.COM

www.ingramcontent.com/pod-product-compliance
Lightning Source LLC
Chambersburg PA
CBHW051538010526
44107CB00064B/2765